The Jungle Book

Rudyard Kipling
Retold by Heather Caldwell

Burlington Books

The Jungle Book

by Rudyard Kipling
Retold by Heather Caldwell

Burlington Books
P. O. Box 54411
3721 Limassol
Cyprus
Burlington Books is an imprint of Danos Books Ltd.

The publisher gratefully acknowledges the following:
Text: *The Jungle Book* by Rudyard Kipling. Adapted by permission of A.P. Watt Ltd. on behalf of The National Trust for Places of Historic Interest or Natural Beauty.
Photographs: Corel Corp.: page 7 (monkey); Getty Images: page 64; Mary Evans Picture Library: page 66; Nova Dev. Co. & licensors: page 7 (tiger, snake, bear, panther); Shutterstock, Inc.: pages 7 (wolf), 14, 40-41, 56, 65

The publisher would like to thank the following people:

Castellano:	Alicia Ruiz Cuéllar
Català:	Maria Esteve Serraviñals
Euskara:	Edurne Azkue Urrestilla
Galego:	Ramón Nicolás Rodríguez

ISBN 978-9963-48-184-2

Burlington Reader No. NE3.05

10 9 8 7 6 5 4 3 2 1
19 18 17 16 15 14 13 12 11 10

CONTENTS

Introducción

Joseph Rudyard Kipling (1865-1936) fue un escritor y poeta británico. Nació en Bombay, en la India británica, pero fue educado en Inglaterra, donde pasó la mayor parte de su vida. En 1894 publicó *El libro de la selva*, que se convirtió en un clásico para los niños de todo el mundo.

El libro cuenta la historia de un niño abandonado en la selva de la India. Una familia de lobos le adopta y le llama Mowgli. El muchacho aprende las leyes de la selva y todas sus lenguas para poder sobrevivir. Pero Mowgli tiene un peligroso enemigo, Shere Khan el tigre. Shere Khan odia a los hombres y quiere matar al "cachorro humano". Los monos, que envidian a Mowgli, le capturan y le llevan a la ciudad perdida, al otro lado de la selva. Los amigos de Mowgli, Baloo el oso, Bagheera la pantera y Kaa la serpiente pitón consiguen rescatarle. Mowgli está otra vez a salvo pero, ¿durante cuánto tiempo?

Introducció

Joseph Rudyard Kipling (1865-1936) va ser un escriptor i poeta britànic. Va néixer a Bombai, a l'Índia britànica, però va ser educat a Anglaterra, on va passar la major part de la seva vida. El 1894 va publicar *El llibre de la selva*, que es va convertir en un clàssic per als nens d'arreu del món.

El llibre explica la història d'un nen abandonat a la selva de l'Índia. Una família de llops l'adopta i li posa el nom de Mowgli. El noi aprèn les lleis de la selva i totes les seves llengües per poder sobreviure. Però en Mowgli té un perillós enemic, Shere Khan, el tigre. Shere Khan odia els homes i vol matar el "cadell humà". Els micos, que envegen en Mowgli, el capturen i el porten a la ciutat perduda, a l'altre costat de la selva. Els amics d'en Mowgli, Baloo, l'ós, Bagheera, la pantera i Kaa, la serp pitó aconsegueixen rescatar-lo. En Mowgli està fora de perill un altre cop, però durant quant de temps?

Sarrera

Joseph Rudyard Kipling (1865-1936) idazle eta poeta britainiarra Bombay-n jaio zen, India britainiarrean, baina Ingalaterran hezi eta igaro zuen bere bizitzako zatirik handiena. 1894an *Oihaneko Liburua* argitaratu zuen, mundu guztiko umeentzat klasiko bihurtu zena.

Indiako oihanean abandonatutako ume baten istorioa kontatzen du ipuinak. Otso-familia batek berekin hartu eta Mowgli ipini dio izena. Mutikoak oihaneko arauak eta hizkuntza guztiak ikasi ditu, bizirik jarraitu ahal izateko. Hala ere, arerio arriskutsu bat du: Shere Khan tigrea. Shere Khanek gorroto ditu gizakiak eta gizakumea hil nahi du. Tximinoek, berriz, inbidia diote eta mutikoa harrapatu eta oihaneko beste muturrean dagoen hiri galdura eraman dute. Mowgliren lagunek, Baloo hartzak, Bagheera panterak eta Kaa sugepitoiak, mutila erreskatatzea lortu dute. Mowgli berriro salbu dago, baina noiz arte?

Limiar

Joseph Rudyard Kipling (1865-1936) foi un escritor e poeta británico. Naceu en Bombai, na India británica, mais foi educado en Inglaterra onde pasou a maior parte da súa vida. En 1894 publicou *O libro da selva*, que se converteu nun clásico para os nenos de todo o mundo.

O libro conta a historia dun neno abandonado na selva da India. Unha familia de lobos adóptao e chámao Mowgli. O rapaz aprende as leis da selva e todas as súas linguas para poder sobrevivir. Mais Mowgli ten un perigoso inimigo, Shere Khan o tigre. Shere Khan odia os homes e quere matar o "cachorro humano". Os monos, que envexan a Mowgli, captúrano e lévano á cidade perdida, ao outro lado da selva. Os amigos de Mowgli, Baloo o oso, Bagheera a pantera e Kaa a serpe pitón conseguen rescatalo, Mowgli está outra vez san e salvo mais, por canto tempo?

CHARACTERS

PRE-READING ACTIVITIES

1 Choose the correct answer.

1. The buffaloes are getting ready to **fight** / **shoot**.
2. You must know how to **tremble** / **survive** in the jungle.
3. If you go into the jungle alone, you will be **wrong** / **in danger**.
4. The **brave** / **frightened** child wasn't afraid of the tiger.
5. The animals have got a lot of respect for their **fear** / **leader**.

2 Match each picture to the correct description.

1. I'm in the dog family.
   I travel and hunt in a group.
   I don't usually attack humans.
2. I eat plants, insects and fish.
   Sometimes, I sleep all winter.
   I have got a large body, a short tail and small ears.
3. I live and hunt alone.
   I'm a very strong climber.
   I'm black with green eyes.
4. I'm a good swimmer.
   I can poison my enemies.
   The sun helps me control my body's temperature.
5. I live in groups.
   I eat fruit, grass and leaves.
   I live mainly in the trees.
6. I hunt at night.
   Humans are my biggest enemy.
   I'm orange, white and black.

CHAPTER 1

The Human Child

A family of wolves lived in a cave in the Seeonee Hills of India. One warm summer evening, the father and mother were sleeping in the cave with their small grey cubs. Suddenly, they heard a loud noise.

"What was that?" asked Mother Wolf.

Father Wolf listened and said, "It's Shere Khan, the tiger. He's hunting tonight."

"Why is he making that loud noise?" Mother Wolf asked. "He'll frighten all the animals."

"He's not hunting an animal," Father Wolf answered. "He's hunting a *human*!"

"Humans? Aren't there enough animals in the forest?" exclaimed Mother Wolf. "Why is he hunting a human? He's always causing problems for us."

"Shere Khan doesn't care about our problems," Father Wolf

answered. "He hunts easy things to catch. Remember Shere Khan can't run fast since he burned his leg in a fire."

Suddenly, a little brown human child ran into the cave. He looked at Father Wolf and laughed.

The big grey wolf was surprised. "It's incredible," he said. "This little human child looks at me and he isn't afraid."

At that moment, Shere Khan, the tiger, **pushed** his big head into the cave. "A human child ran into your cave. I was hunting him. Give him to me now!" he said.

Father Wolf looked at the angry tiger. He wasn't afraid of him because he knew the tiger could only put his head in the cave. He was too big to enter completely.

"Wolves are **free** creatures," Father Wolf said. "We don't have to listen to you, Shere Khan. The child is in our cave and now he belongs to us!"

The tiger was angry. "I **won't argue** with wolves!" he shouted. "Give that child to me now! He's mine!"

Mowgli looked at Father Wolf and laughed.

Mother Wolf looked at the tiger. In the dark cave, her eyes were like two green moons. She wasn't afraid, but she was very angry. "Look at me, Shere Khan. This child is mine!" she said. "He will live in this cave with our family. He will grow up with my cubs and he will run and play with them. You won't have him. You're a big tiger, but you hunt little children. Return to the jungle! Get out of our cave!"

Shere Khan took his head out of the cave and shouted, "You can't keep that human child! You must take him to the Wolf **Council**. The wolf **pack** will give him to me."

Father Wolf was worried. "Shere Khan is right," he said. "It's the wolf pack's decision – not ours. Do you really want to keep this human child, Mother Wolf?"

"Look at this little boy," said Mother Wolf. "He's beautiful. He came to us at night. He was alone, but he wasn't afraid. Look! He's playing with our cubs! That tiger only wants to hurt him because he's a human and he's weak. But we'll keep this little boy. He'll become part of our family. He is like a little frog. Let's call him 'Mowgli the frog'."

Father Wolf looked at the little boy and said, "I hope the Wolf Council will permit us to keep him."

Father and Mother Wolf were good wolves and they knew the **laws** of the jungle. According to these laws, the Wolf Council must accept each new cub. The Council usually accepted all wolf cubs, but Mowgli was a human child, not a wolf.

According to the law of the jungle, animals were not permitted to hunt, or hurt, humans. The animals believed that humans were one of the weakest creatures in the forest because they didn't have **sharp** teeth or **claws** and they didn't run fast, climb high or fly. The animals believed it was not right to hurt these **helpless** creatures.

Father and Mother Wolf waited a long time before they took their cubs and Mowgli to the Council. Every day, they watched their cubs and the boy grow and they knew they couldn't wait forever. Soon, they must meet with the Wolf Council.

What was going to happen to Mowgli?

CHAPTER 2

The Wolf Council

It was the night of the Wolf Council and there was a full moon in the sky. Father and Mother Wolf took their family to the Council Rock, a big hill in the middle of the forest. All the wolves were sitting in a big circle. Akela, the wolf leader, sat on a big rock in the middle of the circle. The wolves sat and watched, and the mothers showed their new babies to the pack. As each mother pushed her cub into the circle, Akela said, "Know the law. Look at our new baby wolves very carefully. These little cubs are the newest members of our pack." All the wolves looked at the cubs. As part of the pack, they were **safe** until they became adult wolves.

Mother Wolf pushed the little boy into the centre of the circle.

Soon, it was Mowgli's turn. Mother Wolf pushed the little boy into the centre of the circle and said, "Meet Mowgli. He's a human, but he's very brave and we love him very much. Can he be part of our pack?"

The big wolves looked at the little brown child. He knew everybody was looking at him, but he was not afraid.

Akela said to the wolves, "Look carefully at the human child. He is now one of us."

There was silence and it seemed Mowgli was safe. Then, suddenly, there was a loud noise and Shere Khan jumped into the middle of the circle. "The human child is mine!" he **roared**. "Give him to me! Wolves don't need a human child. Give me the boy now!"

The wolves wanted to answer this, but they were afraid. According to the law of the jungle, two voices must speak to save Mowgli. All the wolves were afraid of Shere Khan, so they sat in silence. But Mother Wolf was angry and ready to fight them all.

Suddenly, Baloo, the old brown bear, walked into the circle. It was Baloo's job to teach the wolf cubs the laws of the jungle. Because he had a special position, the Wolf Council permitted him to speak. Baloo approached the little boy. He examined him carefully and then said, "This little human child won't hurt anybody. He's small but he's brave. I'll speak for him."

Akela looked at the circle of wolves. "Baloo is voting for Mowgli and we need one more vote," he said.

At that moment, a big black panther jumped into the circle. It was Bagheera. The wolves respected him because he was intelligent and brave. The panther sat down in the middle of the circle. "Can I say something?" he asked.

"Speak!" said the wolves.

"This child is as helpless as a frog," Bagheera said. "We cannot kill the little creature, it is wrong. I've got a big, fat cow not far from here. Let the child live and I'll give you the cow."

One big grey wolf looked at the child and said, "We heard two voices speak to save Mowgli. The child won't hurt us. Let's go and eat the cow."

One by one, the wolves left the Wolf Council. Shere Khan ran back into the forest. He was furious.

Akela, Bagheera, Baloo and the wolf family sat around a big rock. Akela looked at the little boy. "Welcome to our wolf pack, Mowgli.

At that moment, a big black panther jumped into the circle.

Humans have got weak bodies but they have got intelligent minds. One day, maybe you will help us. Until then, you must work hard and study. You must learn all the laws of the jungle, too. You must learn to climb trees and run fast. Shere Khan is a very dangerous enemy, Mowgli. You must always be careful."

Far away in the jungle, there was a horrible noise. It was Shere Khan. That night, he was very angry.

Mowgli was safe, but for how long?

CHAPTERS 1-2 ACTIVITIES

1 Use the letters on the leaves to make words. Then complete the sentences below with the words.

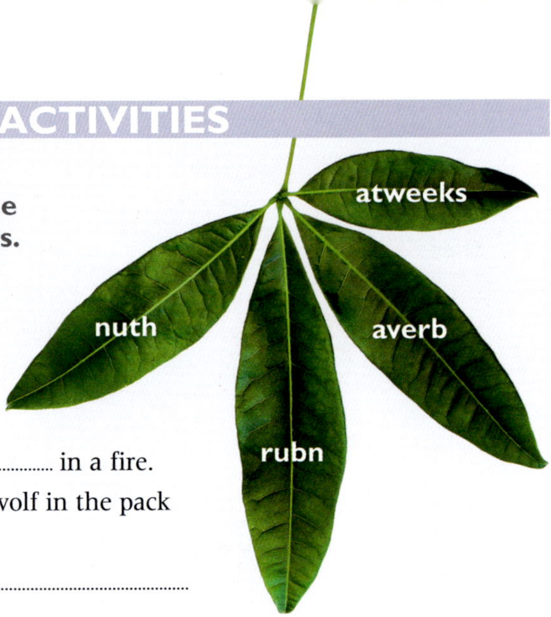

1. Paper will .... in a fire.
2. The .... wolf in the pack won't survive.
3. In the jungle, animals .... for their food.
4. The .... boy jumped on the lion's back.

2 Complete the puzzle.

Across ►

3. to get bigger and bigger
4. to move next to something
5. another word for *appear to be*

Down ▼

1. another word for *combat*
2. members of the dog family
6. We use this to think.

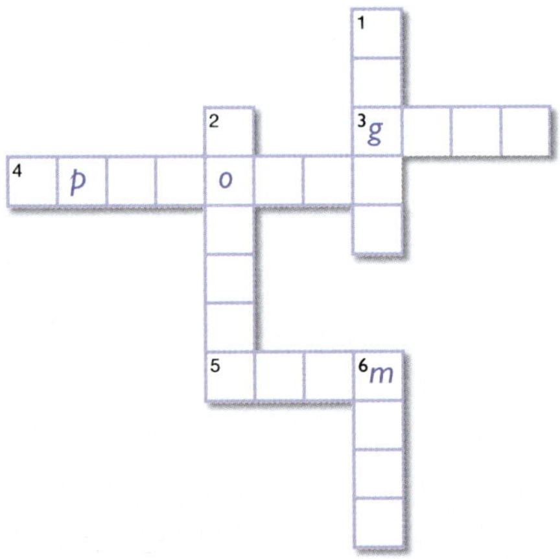

Did you know?

A wolf pack's territory can cover thousands of square kilometres. The wolves use their excellent sense of smell to identify their territory. They've got 200 million nerve cells in their noses to help them identify the source of different smells.

3 Tick (✓) the sentence that is true for each animal.

1. Shere Khan

.... a. He was hunting a human child.
.... b. He was hunting wolves.
.... c. The wolves were hunting him.

2. Mother Wolf

.... a. She was afraid of Shere Khan.
.... b. She wanted to keep Mowgli and let him grow up with her cubs.
.... c. She didn't want Mowgli to stay in the cave with her family.

3. Akela

.... a. He didn't want to accept Mowgli into the wolf pack.
.... b. Mowgli was afraid of him.
.... c. He welcomed Mowgli to the wolf pack.

4. Bagheera

.... a. He gave the wolves a cow to save Mowgli's life.
.... b. Shere Khan tried to fight him.
.... c. The wolves had no respect for him.

4 Answer the questions. Write the answers in your notebook.

1. Why was Father Wolf surprised when Mowgli ran into the cave?
2. Why were the wolves in the cave safe from Shere Khan?
3. How did Mowgli get his name?
4. What was the law of the jungle about hunting humans?
5. Who was Baloo? What was his job?
6. According to Bagheera, why shouldn't the animals kill Mowgli?

CHAPTER 3

Mowgli Meets the Monkeys

Mowgli lived happily with his wolf family in the jungle. Father Wolf taught the boy to listen to the wind and rain. Soon, Mowgli knew everything a wolf must know to survive in the jungle. Now, it was time for him to study with Baloo, the bear.

Baloo taught all the young animals in the forest. He loved young Mowgli because he was very intelligent. He wanted to teach the human child all the languages of the jungle. Unfortunately, the lessons weren't always fun for Mowgli. He hated practising his new words and Baloo was sometimes an impatient teacher. Mowgli was still a child and he wanted to have fun and play games.

Another group of animals lived in the jungle and they also wanted to have fun and play games. They were the monkeys.

The monkeys were very curious about the human child in the jungle. They wanted to meet him, but they didn't have an opportunity because Mowgli was never alone. He was usually with his wolf family, or learning with Baloo. The monkeys waited patiently for their opportunity. Finally, it arrived.

One day, they were watching the boy having a difficult lesson with Baloo. They heard Mowgli shout angrily and run to the river to play. "Yes!" they **whispered**. "The human child is alone now. Come, brothers. Let's go and meet him!"

The monkeys heard Mowgli shout angrily and run to the river to play.

The monkeys quickly **surrounded** the surprised boy. They smiled at him in a friendly way and he smiled, too. Encouraged, they took him up into the trees and gave him delicious fruit and **nuts**. They played games with him in the trees and had fun. Mowgli liked his new friends.

Down on the **ground**, under the trees, Baloo received a visit from Bagheera, the black panther. "Good afternoon, Baloo," said Bagheera. "Where is Mowgli? Isn't this your lesson time?"

Baloo looked at Bagheera and said, "Your little friend is hiding in the trees again. He's angry."

Bagheera looked worried. "Did you hit Mowgli?" he asked.

"No," the old bear said. "He didn't want to learn his lessons, so he ran to the river to play."

The black panther looked sad for a moment. "Don't make the boy work so hard," he said. "He's just a child and he should have some fun."

Baloo **turned** to the panther. "Mowgli is getting older, Bagheera. He's a human. He must learn to protect himself in the jungle. If the human child can't protect himself, he will never survive. Right now, I'm teaching Mowgli all the languages of the jungle.

If Mowgli can talk with the animals, he will be safe most of the time."

Suddenly, they heard a happy voice from the tree. "Bagheera, my good friend!" Mowgli shouted and jumped from the tree. He looked at the big bear, angrily. "Baloo, I don't want any more lessons today."

Baloo smiled at the human child. "Tell our friend, Bagheera, the new words I taught you today, Mowgli," he said.

"Which words do you want to hear? I know a lot of languages," laughed Mowgli. He forgot he was angry with Baloo. The boy loved showing the animals he was very intelligent.

Mowgli spent the next half an hour speaking all the different languages of the jungle. Baloo was very **proud** of his young pupil.

"Our little friend is a good student," Bagheera whispered. "But we mustn't forget Shere Khan. He will always be Mowgli's enemy."

Mowgli jumped on the panther's back. "Hey, Bagheera! I made some new friends today."

"What?" asked Bagheera. "What new friends?"

"I ran away from Baloo because he was impatient with me and I was angry. Then, the big grey monkeys came down from the trees. They were very friendly. They took me up in the trees and gave me nice things to eat. I want to live in their tribe with them," Mowgli smiled.

But Bagheera didn't smile. He was angry. "Listen to me, Mowgli. You can't **trust** the monkeys. They are bad and they tell lies," he said.

Mowgli began to cry. "That's not true!" he shouted. "The monkeys are kind. I want to live with them and play all day. They don't have to learn all the stupid laws of the jungle. They don't have to learn languages and have lessons – they just have fun."

Then, Baloo spoke. He was very angry and his voice was like thunder. "Listen boy, and listen carefully. The monkeys haven't got laws to help them **behave** correctly. They are stupid and cruel. They throw rocks at animals to hurt them and then, they laugh at their pain."

Bagheera looked at the bear and asked, "Baloo, did you tell Mowgli to **stay away** from the monkeys?"

Baloo **shook his head**. "No. I was busy teaching Mowgli the languages of the jungle," he answered. "I didn't tell him about the monkeys."

"Stupid bear!" the panther shouted. "You forgot to tell Mowgli

"Stupid bear!" the panther shouted. "You forgot to tell Mowgli about one of the biggest dangers in the jungle!"

about one of the biggest dangers in the jungle!"

Then, Bagheera turned to Mowgli. "This is important, Mowgli," he said, in a very serious voice. "Stay away from the monkeys! They are dirty and horrible. Don't talk to them, don't play with them and don't eat their food."

Mowgli was perplexed. The little boy loved Bagheera and Baloo but he didn't understand their **anger**. In his opinion, the monkeys were great fun and enjoyed their life. What was so terrible about that?

Up in the trees, the monkeys were talking. "The human child is intelligent," one grey monkey said. "Maybe he can teach us to build houses. Let's try and capture Mowgli and make him part of our tribe."

All the monkeys agreed with this decision: they must capture Mowgli and take him to the Lost City at the other side of the jungle.

Quietly, they followed Baloo, Bagheera and Mowgli to their side of the forest. Then, they hid in the trees and waited until the three friends **fell asleep** in the afternoon sun.

CHAPTER 4

Problems for Mowgli

Mowgli, Baloo and Bagheera were sleeping happily under the tree. Suddenly, four monkeys surrounded Mowgli and picked him up. They took him up to the top of the trees. Mowgli tried to call for help, but the monkeys were too quick for him. By the time his friends opened their eyes, Mowgli was high up in the trees. They couldn't help the young boy now. Mowgli heard the monkeys laughing at his friends. "Baloo was right," he thought. "The monkeys are horrible. They laugh at other animals' problems."

The monkeys jumped from tree to tree with Mowgli in their arms. They passed him from monkey to monkey. High up in the sky, the boy could see the entire jungle and the little villages down on the ground.

The monkeys jumped from tree to tree with Mowgli in their arms.

Mowgli wanted to send a message to his friends, but he didn't know a way to do it. Suddenly, he saw an eagle and remembered his bird language. "Go and find Baloo, the bear!" he shouted to the eagle. "The monkeys took me and Baloo must save me from them."

"Who are you, little brother?" asked the eagle.

"I am Mowgli," he answered. "I am the human child."

The eagle flew back into the forest and went to look for Baloo.

Back in the forest, Baloo and Bagheera were very worried. Baloo lay on the ground, crying. "I am the saddest bear in the jungle! Oh, Mowgli! Why didn't you believe me about the cruel monkeys?"

Bagheera looked at the bear and said, "Baloo, stop crying and get up! You taught the boy well. Trust Mowgli – he's intelligent. Now, let's make a plan. We must go and rescue Mowgli."

Baloo stopped crying and sat up. "Let's go to our friend, Kaa, the python. That snake is the monkeys' worst enemy. Kaa is old, intelligent and very hungry. His big eyes can hypnotise them. Kaa will be happy to help us, especially if we promise him a good meal," he said.

Soon, Baloo and Bagheera found the enormous python. He was sleeping in the sun. Kaa was ready for a big meal. He looked at the bear and the panther. "Hello, friends," he said. "Why are you here?"

"We are hunting," said Baloo. "Do you want to come with us?"

"Yes, I'll come with you, I'm very hungry," said Kaa. "There aren't any monkeys in the forest today. Where are they all?"

"The monkeys went on a long journey through the jungle," said Bagheera. "We heard them. They were laughing about a big yellow **worm** named Kaa."

Kaa became angry. "Did they really call me a *worm*?" he shouted. "They will never laugh at Kaa, the great python, again!"

Bagheera spoke quietly. "We are also angry with the monkeys. They stole our human child, Mowgli."

Kaa's eyes were burning like fire. "Take me to the monkeys," he said. "I will teach them a lesson and they will never forget it."

Bagheera and Baloo smiled. "If we help you find the monkeys, will you help us fight them?" Baloo asked.

The great python **nodded his head**. "**With pleasure**," he said, in a sinister voice.

Soon, Baloo and Bagheera found the enormous python.

CHAPTERS 3-4 ACTIVITIES

1 Write Y (yes) or N (no) next to each sentence.

1. If you walk **quietly**, do you make a lot of noise? ....
2. Has a **busy** person got a lot of time to drink coffee and talk to friends? ....
3. Can a **journey** take more than a day? ....
4. Is it good to feel **encouraged**? ....
5. If somebody likes **telling lies**, will you believe him? ....

2 Match each sentence in A to a sentence in B to make a logical pair.

A

1. I don't **agree** with the new law.
2. I can't find a **way** to explain this word.
3. I've got a **pain** in my back.
4. The child **ran away** from me.

B

.... a. I'll look in the dictionary.
.... b. It's difficult for me to move.
.... c. He was frightened.
.... d. It's very unjust.

3 Match each character with an action.

a. lies on the ground and cries

b. calls Baloo a stupid bear

c. shouts angrily and runs to the river to play

d. decides to teach the monkeys a lesson

4 Answer the questions. Write the answers in your notebook.

1. Why was it difficult for the monkeys to meet Mowgli?
2. Why did Bagheera shout at Baloo?
3. How did Mowgli react after Bagheera explained about the monkeys?
4. Why did the monkeys want to capture Mowgli?
5. Why did Mowgli change his opinion of the monkeys?
6. Why did Baloo ask Kaa to help rescue Mowgli?

Did you know?

Many people differentiate between a black bear and a brown bear. But colour is never an indicator of species. "Black" bears and "brown" bears might have other colours, from almost white to pure black. The differences in colour depend on age, sex and the climate.

CHAPTER 5

The Battle with the Monkeys

There was a noise high up in the trees. Baloo, Kaa and Bagheera looked up and saw a big eagle. He was calling to them. "Up! Up! Look up, Baloo the bear! Mowgli, the human child, sends you a message: the monkeys took him. You must save him. Maybe the monkeys are taking him to the Lost City. Good hunting to you all."

"Good hunting to you, Eagle," said Bagheera. Then, he turned to Baloo. "Mowgli remembered his lessons. You taught him the languages of the jungle and he talked to the eagle. We must find him quickly. Come, let's begin our journey."

Together, the panther, the bear and the snake began to travel to the Lost City.

The Lost City was a secret place in the dark jungle. Long ago, it was a big, beautiful city with stone palaces and big houses, and humans lived there. But the people left the city and forgot about it. Soon, the city became part of the jungle.

The monkeys started to use the abandoned city, making their homes in the empty houses. They sat in the ruined buildings and **pretended** they were humans. They ran in the gardens and threw fruit and flowers from the trees to the ground.

*****

The monkeys finally arrived at the Lost City. Most animals in the jungle rested after a long journey, but the monkeys were different. They danced in a circle and sang stupid songs.

Mowgli thought they were behaving very strangely. "I want to eat," he said to them. "I'm a stranger in this part of the jungle and I'm hungry. Please bring me some food or let me hunt."

"Food! Food! The child wants food! Let's get him some food!" shouted a group of monkeys. They ran to get Mowgli some fruit and nuts, but before they could find any, they began to fight. Poor Mowgli was tired and hungry. He wanted to go home to his cave and his family. "Baloo and Bagheera were right," he thought. "These stupid monkeys haven't got any laws or any leaders. They sing stupid songs and dance. They steal, fight and are very cruel. I must find a way to go home."

Mowgli tried to find a way out of the city, but the monkeys were watching him. Each time he approached the city walls, they stopped him. "Don't leave us, boy," they said. "You're very lucky because you're with us now. We are the most intelligent animals in the jungle."

Mowgli didn't answer. He followed the monkeys to a building in the centre of the city. It didn't have a **roof** but it had high stone walls. Mowgli lay on the ground and tried to sleep, but the monkeys didn't leave him alone.

The monkeys didn't leave Mowgli alone.

One big monkey shouted at him, "Listen, boy! You must stay with us. We are wonderful. Listen to our words, then return to your friends in the jungle and tell them about the wonderful monkeys. We have fun all day and all night."

Mowgli was very tired. "Don't these stupid animals sleep?" he thought. Mowgli looked at the sky and saw big clouds. "It's the end of the day and it will be dark soon. When it's dark, I'll run away. But now I'm too tired."

CHAPTER 6

Kaa Saves Mowgli

Mowgli didn't know it, but outside the walls of the city, Baloo, Bagheera and Kaa were making plans. "I will go to the ruined buildings in the centre of the city," said Bagheera. "I want to see if the monkeys are planning something."

"As soon as you need me, I will begin to fight," Baloo said.

"I'll come last and surprise them," the snake whispered. "Good hunting, friends."

Baloo, Bagheera and Kaa moved silently into the Lost City. Suddenly, Bagheera jumped over the wall and the battle began. Mowgli couldn't help Bagheera because the monkeys carried him to another building and pushed him inside. Mowgli fell three metres onto a cold stone floor. He heard the fighting through the broken wall, but he couldn't get out.

Bagheera jumped over the wall and the battle began.

"You stay here and watch this!" shouted the monkeys. "We're going to kill your friends."

Mowgli heard Bagheera fighting for his life. Mowgli wanted to help him, but he couldn't – he was also in danger. Many **poisonous** snakes lived inside the old building. Luckily, Mowgli remembered the snake language and he talked to them. "We're brothers," he said to the snakes. "Please, don't hurt me."

"Don't move, little brother," said the snakes. "Be careful. Don't hurt our babies with your big feet." Mowgli knew he was safe for now, but what about Bagheera?

Then, Mowgli had an idea. "Bagheera, try and go to the water tanks!" he shouted. "Monkeys don't like water!"

Bagheera heard him and suddenly felt stronger because he knew Mowgli was **alive**. Slowly, he fought his way to the water tanks and jumped inside. Then, he heard a loud noise. Baloo, the bear was joining the battle. The big bear attacked as many monkeys as he could. The monkeys were now busy fighting Baloo. They didn't see Kaa until he was in the middle of the battle and then, there was silence. The monkeys weren't frightened of lions, tigers or bears, but they were terrified of snakes. The great python was more than ten metres long, and Kaa was the most dangerous animal in the jungle for the monkeys. They couldn't look into his big eyes because he could hypnotise them and then kill them all.

The big bear attacked as many monkeys as he could.

The monkeys began to run away into the forest. Kaa **raised** his head. His eyes were burning. The monkeys looked into his eyes, then stopped running and stood like statues. Baloo stood up and Bagheera climbed out of the water tank. The monkeys didn't look at them. They were all looking at Kaa. He was hypnotising them with his magic eyes.

"Quick! We must save Mowgli before the monkeys hurt him," said Bagheera.

"The monkeys won't hurt anybody now," whispered Kaa in a quiet, sinister voice. "They can't move until I let them."

"My body hurts," said Baloo. "Those monkeys can fight! Mowgli! Where are you?"

"I'm here!" shouted Mowgli. "I'm in this old building. I can't get out!"

"Please, get this boy out of our house!" shouted the snakes. "His feet are dangerous. We're afraid he'll stand on our babies."

Kaa smiled and said to Baloo, "Your boy, Mowgli, is a good student. He **even** makes friends with the snakes." Kaa turned his head and called to Mowgli. "Stay away from the wall, child. I'll break it with my head."

Kaa raised his great body off the ground and broke the stone wall with his giant head. At last, Mowgli was free! The boy returned to Baloo and Bagheera. Then, he saw the great python's head. "So, *you* are the great Kaa. We are brothers. My food is your food. If you are hungry in the future, I will help you."

"Thank you, little brother," said Kaa. "But what animal can you kill? You're still a little boy."

“I won’t kill anything because I am little,” answered Mowgli. “But one day, I’ll be a great hunter and I’ll bring you food. Good hunting to you, my big brother.”

Baloo and Kaa were very impressed by Mowgli’s words. “The human child has got a brave heart and a quick mind,” said Kaa. “One day, he will be a great man. Now, it is time for all of you to go. I’m very hungry.”

The monkeys heard Kaa’s words and began to tremble. They knew something horrible was going to happen. The long python began to dance in strange circles. Mowgli looked around. All the animals, including Baloo and Bagheera, were looking at Kaa without moving. Mowgli put his hands on his friends and they jumped. They woke up from their hypnosis and were afraid.

“What’s the problem?” asked Mowgli. “It’s only a snake dancing in circles.”

“We must get out of here quickly,” said Bagheera. “Kaa is getting ready to eat. The monkeys are in danger now.”

The three friends quickly ran into the jungle. Mowgli climbed on Bagheera’s back and fell asleep. He didn’t wake again until he was safe in Mother Wolf’s cave.

All the animals, including Baloo and Bagheera, were looking at Kaa without moving.

CHAPTERS 5-6 ACTIVITIES

1 Match each word to the correct definition.

1. leave alone
2. long ago
3. impressed
4. heart
5. in danger
6. rest

..... a. not do physical work

..... b. don't look at or talk to; don't give attention to

..... c. many years before, in the past

..... d. an important organ in the body

..... e. caused admiration

..... f. at risk

2 Complete each sentence with a word / words from activity 1.

1. I don't remember you because we met ....
2. You look tired. You should ....
3. You speak ten languages! I'm very ....
4. The child isn't afraid of anything. He's got a brave ....
5. Be careful! Your life is ....
6. Please, ... me .... I don't want visitors.

Did you know?

If a python is hungry, it will wait for its victim and then capture it in its strong mouth. It uses its long body to hold the victim very firmly, then the snake eats the animal in one piece. After it eats an animal it can go without food for weeks or months.

3 Write a sentence for each picture. Use the names from A, a phrase from B and and a phrase from C.

A	B	C
1. **Mowgli**	attacked	a lot of monkeys.
2. **The Lost City**	returned to	in the jungle.
3. **Bagheera**	tried to sleep	over the wall.
4. **Baloo**	jumped	on the ground.
5. **Mowgli**	was getting ready	Baloo and Bagheera.
6. **Kaa**	was a secret place	to eat.

4 Answer the questions. Write the answers in your notebook.

1. What was the eagle's message to Baloo?
2. Why couldn't Mowgli help his friends fight against the monkeys?
3. What did Mowgli shout to Bagheera? Why?
4. Why couldn't the monkeys run away into the forest?
5. How did Kaa help Mowgli get out of the old building?
6. What was Kaa's opinion of Mowgli?

CHAPTER 7

The Red Flowers

Five years passed and Mowgli was happy in the jungle. He enjoyed hunting with his wolf brothers. On hot afternoons, he swam in the cool rivers and then slept in the sun. Life was good for the young boy. He had food, friends, family and a safe home. But Shere Khan still hated the human child. While Mowgli was growing bigger and stronger, the tiger was busy making plans.

Shere Khan always remembered the night of the council meeting. He was still angry with Akela, the wolf leader, for not giving him the child. Now, the **evil** tiger wanted to kill both Mowgli and Akela. Shere Khan was waiting for the day that Akela became too old and weak to hunt a **deer**. According to the laws of the jungle, the wolves in the pack kill the wolf leader when he is too weak to hunt a deer.

The old tiger made friends with the young wolves. "Come, let me **share** my meat with you," said Shere Khan. "I've got some news from the jungle."

The young wolves ate the meat happily and listened to Shere Khan.

The tiger whispered, "I hear the animals in the jungle talking. They're laughing at the wolves. They think it's funny your leader is old and weak and you permit a human child to live with you."

"Mowgli is part of the pack," said one wolf. "Remember, it's death to kill a brother."

"True. But why is that human child a member of your pack?" asked the tiger. "Twelve years ago, not one wolf defended him at the Wolf Council. The black panther Bagheera exchanged a cow for the life of the child. Now, the child is almost a man, and one day he will hunt you."

"But Akela protects him," said another wolf.

"Ah, that's true, but Akela will die, and then you can give him to me. One of you can be the leader of the pack instead," said the tiger. "**Let's make a deal.** I'll help you kill Akela, and you'll give Mowgli to me."

The young wolves agreed to the evil tiger's plan.

*****

The young wolves ate the meat happily and listened to Shere Khan.

One day, Akela was hunting a deer. Suddenly, Shere Khan ran into his **path** and the deer escaped. Akela couldn't kill it. The young wolves were happy and wanted to kill their leader immediately, but Shere Khan said, "Wait until the next Wolf Council. I'll help you kill Akela then."

Suddenly, Shere Khan ran into Akela's path and the deer escaped.

Fortunately, Bagheera the panther heard them and went to look for Mowgli in the jungle. "Mowgli," he said, "you must prepare yourself for the next Wolf Council. Your life is in danger!"

The boy laughed and said, "From Shere Khan? Don't worry. That old tiger can't hurt me. I'm more intelligent than he is. I know how to **take care of** myself, and my wolf friends will protect me."

Bagheera shook his head. "Mowgli, it isn't just Shere Khan," he said. It's also the wolf pack. Shere Khan made friends with the young wolves. Now, they hate you because of that evil tiger. Remember, you're a human and they're wolves. You're different to them."

"Bagheera, what can I do?" asked Mowgli.

"Listen carefully," said the panther. "You're not stronger than them, but you're much more intelligent. Do you know about the red flowers?"

"The red flowers? What are they?" asked Mowgli.

"That's the animal description for fire. Humans use it to keep their houses warm and to cook food. All the animals in the forest are afraid of fire, because they don't know how to use it," Bagheera continued. "Mowgli, you're a human, and you can learn to use it. You must go to the villages of men and steal some fire for the next Wolf Council meeting."

Mowgli followed the panther's advice. He went to the villages and watched the women cooking on fires. He learned how to make fire and how to use it. Mowgli stole some red-hot **coals** in an iron pot. Now, he was ready for the Wolf Council meeting.

Mowgli stole some red-hot coals in an iron pot.

CHAPTER 8

A Frightening Plan

On the night of the council, Akela lay on a big rock. He watched all the wolves come together. One group stood behind Shere Khan. Akela spoke to the pack, "Tonight we're having a special meeting. As you all know, I didn't kill the deer at the last hunt. That means that today you must choose a new leader. One of you will fight me for my position. Before the battle ... "

Suddenly, Shere Khan shouted, "Don't **waste** time listening to this old fool! Soon, he'll be dead. There's a bigger danger in the pack ... Mowgli, the human child. He'll bring danger to the wolves. Give me Mowgli, and I'll help you kill Akela."

One wolf shouted, "We don't want humans in our forest! Send the boy back to his people."

Shere Khan laughed. "The boy will return to his people and tell them all your secrets. Don't be stupid! The boy must die tonight!"

The wolves got up and moved next to Shere Khan. Mowgli stood up like a man and looked at the wolves. "For 12 years, I was part of your pack," he said to them. "I ate, played and ran with you all. I took **thorns** from your **paws**. I helped you escape from animal traps. Now, suddenly, I'm your enemy because I'm a human, and you're ready to kill me. But look here! I've got a surprise for you."

Mowgli put a stick in the pot of coals and waited until it began to burn. Suddenly, the boy stood in front of the wolves, holding a torch. He held it high above his head. The wolves began to shout and

hid their eyes. They were terrified of the fire. Mowgli could smell their fear.

Mowgli laughed. "Look at you! You aren't brave wolves, you're noisy dogs. I don't want to live among dogs ... I'll go now and return to the world of humans."

Holding the burning torch, Mowgli watched Shere Khan. The big tiger walked slowly towards him. He was ready for a battle.

Mowgli touched the tiger's head with the torch. Shere Khan roared in pain, and then ran into the jungle.

Mowgli looked at the pack of wolves and said, "I'm leaving the jungle now. But listen to my words and remember them! I am still part of the jungle. I'll watch all of you from far away. Don't hurt my dear friend, Akela. I'll kill you if you try to do this."

Mowgli could see the red light of the fire shining in all the wolves' eyes. It looked like red flowers. Slowly, Mowgli turned and walked out of the forest. It was time for him to go to the world of humans.

Holding the burning torch,
Mowgli watched Shere Khan.

CHAPTERS 7-8 ACTIVITIES

1 Circle the correct answer.

1. Which word describes a horror film?
   a. funny b. frightening
2. Which gives light?
   a. a torch b. a flower
3. Which is more sociable?
   a. to live alone b. to live among friends
4. Which is more dangerous to a wolf?
   a. an iron pot b. an animal trap

2 Choose the correct answer to complete the sentences. Pay attention to the words in bold.

1. If you need **advice**, it's a good idea to ...
   a. ask a friend for help. b. look in a dictionary.
2. The flowers are **dead**, so ...
   a. you should give them water. b. you should buy new flowers.
3. Many people have got a **fear** of ...
   a. cows. b. snakes.
4. You can use a **stick** to ...
   a. help you walk. b. write a story.
5. If a place is **noisy**, ...
   a. it's difficult to have a conversation. b. you mustn't go there alone.
6. I **smell** something delicious. I think ...
   a. there's food cooking on the fire. b. my head hurts.

3 Tick (✓) the things that happened in the story.

1

2

3

4

5

6

4 Answer the questions. Write the answers in your notebook.

1. What was the law of the jungle for the wolf leader?
2. What deal did Shere Khan make with the young wolves?
3. Why didn't Akela kill the deer?
4. What was Bagheera's advice to Mowgli?
5. Why was Mowgli angry with the wolves? Explain in your own words.
6. Why were the wolves afraid of Mowgli?

Did you know?

Fire was important to the evolution of early humans. It helped them cook food and stay active into the night hours and it protected them from animals.

CHAPTER 9

Life in the Village

Mowgli started to walk away from the jungle. He knew he had many enemies among the wolves and he wanted to be far from the jungle. Mowgli walked for a long time until he came to a valley. He could see young boys taking care of the cows and buffaloes. The young boys saw Mowgli and ran quickly towards their home in Kanhiwara Village. Mowgli followed them, but he didn't enter the village because he was afraid.

"This is interesting," Mowgli thought. "The animals in the jungle are afraid of men, but men are also afraid of them."

The boy sat outside the **gate** and waited until finally a man opened it. Mowgli stood up and pointed to his mouth to show he was hungry. The man looked at him and ran away. Everybody in the village came to see the wild boy from the jungle. The people shouted and pointed at him. Mowgli stood quietly and said to himself, "These people are noisy and they haven't got any **manners**! They're just like the grey monkeys!"

The village priest came to examine the strange boy. "Why are you afraid?" the priest asked the people. "He's just a boy. Look at these cuts on his arms and legs. This little boy grew up with the wolves of the forest!"

The women in the village came to look at Mowgli. One woman touched his face and said, "Poor child, he's very thin, and his face and hands are very dirty. Look, Messua, he's just like your son!"

Everybody in the village came to see the wild boy from the jungle.

Messua was a pretty woman with long black hair. She looked at the boy and remembered. Once she had a beautiful little boy. One day, he was playing in the forest with the village children when suddenly, a tiger appeared. The other children ran away, but her little boy could not run fast. Nobody saw her son again. And now, this wild boy appeared from the jungle. Was he her son?

"Let me see him," said Messua. "No, he's not my son – he's too tall and thin. But wait ... he looks a little like him."

The village priest was an intelligent man. He knew Messua was the wife of one of the richest men in the village. He looked up at the sky, pointed at the boy and said, "Messua, the jungle took your baby in the past, and now it gives you this handsome young boy. Take him home, clean him and give him good food. Help him to be a human boy again."

Messua took Mowgli home. She gave him warm milk and bread. Then, she put her hand on his face and looked into his eyes. She tried to see her little son in this thin, wild boy. She called him by her son's name. "Nathos?" But Mowgli did not react to the name. She tried again. "Nathos, I bought you your first shoes. Do you remember them?"

Messua put her hand on his face and looked into his eyes.

Messua touched Mowgli's foot. It was as hard as a rock. "This isn't Nathos. This foot didn't wear a shoe," she said. But then she looked at the boy and he smiled at her. She decided to keep him and love him.

First of all, Messua decided, Mowgli must learn to speak the language of humans. Messua said a word and Mowgli repeated it immediately. Soon, he learned the names of everything in the house and Messua was happy. But at bedtime, Mowgli became nervous. He didn't like sleeping inside a house and he was afraid of the bed. Messua's husband said, "Let the boy sleep outside. I'm sure he won't run away."

Mowgli went to sleep outside. Before he closed his eyes, a **soft** grey nose touched his face. It was one of his wolf brothers. "Wake up, little brother. I bring news," he said.

A soft grey nose touched Mowgli's face.

Mowgli sat up. "What is happening in the jungle?" he said. "How is our family?"

"Everybody is well. You burned Shere Khan very badly. I'm afraid he'll kill you when he returns," said his brother.

"I'll kill him first!" said Mowgli.

"Little brother, don't forget you're a wolf," said his brother.

"Never! I'll always love my wolf family, but not the wolf pack. They wanted to kill me," said Mowgli. "I can't forget that."

"Brother, you'll always be part of our cave," said his brother. "But be careful of men. They talk like monkeys and their words have got no meaning. We'll stay in contact. I'll continue bringing you news of the family." He touched Mowgli with his nose and then disappeared into the night.

CHAPTER 10

Mowgli Tries to Be a Human Boy

For the next three months, Mowgli did not leave the village. He was busy learning how to be a human boy, sleep in a bed and wear clothes. It wasn't easy. The bed was hot and uncomfortable. He slept near the window because he wanted to look at the stars. He wasn't accustomed to wearing clothes. In the village, he wore clothes all the time, but he didn't like it. Shoes hurt his feet and he couldn't run fast in trousers. There were also a lot of stupid rules, and they **didn't make sense** to the boy.

In the jungle, he could eat when he was hungry and sleep when he was tired. In the human world, there were special times for eating and sleeping. Baths were another problem. In the forest, he bathed in the rivers and **streams**. In the human world, people only washed in a bath. But the most confusing thing was the idea of status and power. In the forest, strong animals like the wolf, bear, leopard and snake were the most powerful animals. In the human world, physical **strength** was not important. Money gave status and power to people.

Mowgli wasn't accustomed to wearing clothes.

According to the humans, money could make a man strong or weak. Mowgli thought to himself, "Why is money so important? You can't eat or drink money. It can't make you run faster or jump higher." But Mowgli watched and learned. He saw rich people were powerful and poor people were weak.

Mowgli also noticed humans spent a lot of time telling stupid stories. The animals in the forest did not waste words. The wolves only used words for important messages. They did not invent songs or sing and dance. Only the monkeys had time for such stupid things and no creature in the jungle respected the monkeys. However, humans liked singing, dancing and telling stories. Every evening the people met in the village square to hear stories of the jungle. Buldeo, the village hunter, told them stories about the intelligent monkeys and the stupid bears. Mowgli tried not to laugh, because he knew the stories were not true.

Then, one day, Buldeo told them a story about a tiger.

"The big yellow tiger is the strongest and most intelligent animal in the jungle. He's the king of all the animals. The bear, the panther and the snake all follow his orders. Man is afraid of him because he sometimes comes down to our village to steal our small children."

Mowgli knew Buldeo's words were false, so he spoke for the first time. "You're wrong! The tiger isn't the king of all the animals. He's just another animal in the forest. Most good animals don't like the tiger because he's evil!"

Buldeo became very angry. He shouted, "Oh, the jungle boy can speak! What do you know? Did you hunt a wolf or a tiger? That old tiger is stronger and more intelligent than you are!"

Mowgli shouted back, "Stupid man! You know nothing of the jungle! Maybe that tiger is stronger, but I'm much more intelligent than he is!"

Buldeo's face became red. He was very angry and he could hardly speak. "Do you think you're intelligent? So kill that tiger and bring me his tail. The British pay 100 rupees for a tiger's tail."

The people in the village were angry because Mowgli shouted at Buldeo. The leader of the village said, "This boy is too big to sit around the village. He must work like the other boys."

So Mowgli began to work with the village boys. His job was to take care of the cows and buffaloes, and Mowgli was happy.

"You're wrong! The tiger isn't the king of all the animals," said Mowgli.

CHAPTERS 9-10 ACTIVITIES

1 **Write the correct word under each picture. Then use the words to complete the sentences below.**

valley *point* *priest* *tail* *bath*

A 
....

B 
....

C 
....

D 
....

E 
....

1. The .... sat quietly in the church.
2. "Please have a .... before you go to sleep," Mother said.
3. Can you .... to the country on the map?
4. My dog has got long ears and a short ....
5. Let's walk into the .... between the two mountains.

2 **Use the words below to complete the sentences.**

follow orders *cuts* *sure* *power* *notice*

1. Are you .... these are yours?
2. They learned to .... from their leader.
3. The leader of the pack has got the most ....
4. Did you .... the strange writing on the wall?
5. The boy fell on the rocks. He has got many .... on his leg.

3 Who said it? Write the number of the correct character next to each sentence.

Mowgli

Messua

the priest

Buldeo

the wolf brother

..... a. Take him home, clean him and give him good food.

..... b. Nathos, I bought you your first shoes. Do you remember them?

..... c. We'll stay in contact. I'll continue bringing you news of the family.

..... d. The big yellow tiger is the strongest and most intelligent animal in the jungle.

..... e. Maybe that tiger is strong, but I'm much more intelligent than he is!

4 Answer the questions. Write the answers in your notebook.

1. Why couldn't Mowgli enter the village?
2. What was Mowgli's opinion of the people from the village?
3. Why did Messua agree to take care of Mowgli?
4. What news did Mowgli's wolf brother give him?
5. Name three things Mowgli did not like about life in the village.
6. According to Mowgli, what was the most confusing thing about the human world?

Did You know?

The tiger is one of the most hunted animals in the world. Its body parts have got many different uses. Today, the price of a tiger's body is about €20,000. People in China use the tiger's tail to help treat skin cancer.

CHAPTER 11

Mowgli's New Job

Mowgli was sitting on the back of the biggest, strongest buffalo.

On the first day of his new job, Mowgli met the other boys in the village. Mowgli was sitting on the back of the biggest, strongest buffalo. "**From now on**, I'm the leader," he declared. Mowgli was the strongest boy in the village, so the other boys didn't argue. He was different and they were afraid of him.

"You boys take the cows up into the hills," said Mowgli. "I'll take the buffaloes to the river. We'll meet at the gate at the end of the day." The boys obeyed. Mowgli took his buffaloes down to the Wainganga River. The river was next to the jungle. While his animals were eating the sweet grass, Mowgli went into the jungle to find his wolf brother.

"Mowgli, I've got bad news for you," his brother said. "Shere Khan returned to the jungle. You're in great danger again."

"Don't worry, I've got a plan," said Mowgli. "I'm ready for the tiger, but I will need your help."

"Of course I'll help you. Every day I'll come and bring you news," said the wolf. Then, the grey wolf disappeared silently into the forest.

Many days passed and Mowgli enjoyed working with the animals. Every day he took the buffaloes to the river. While the animals were resting quietly in the river, the boy met one of his wolf brothers. He gave him news of the forest. One day, his wolf brother had some bad news.

"Shere Khan knows you're here. He's going to attack you tomorrow. You must be ready for him," said the wolf.

"Listen to my plan," said Mowgli. "My buffaloes haven't got sharp teeth or claws, but they are big strong animals. Sometimes, they're afraid, and then they **stampede**. In that case, buffaloes are more dangerous than any other animal in the jungle. We'll wait until Shere Khan comes to the river. Then, you'll frighten the buffaloes and start a stampede towards the river. Once the buffaloes are in the river, Shere Khan can't escape. The sides of the river are high. If Shere Khan is in the river, he won't be able to escape the stampede. But we need another wolf. Two wolves must start the stampede. Can you call another wolf brother?"

"That's not a problem," said the wolf. He **howled** loudly and suddenly, a giant wolf appeared.

"Akela! You're here!" shouted Mowgli. He ran to greet his friend.

"Little human, you saved my life," said Akela. "Now, I'll save yours."

Then, his wolf brother said, "Look, the sun is going down in the sky. You must go home. We will meet at the Wainganga River tomorrow. Goodbye, little brother."

"I'm ready," said Mowgli. "You will run after my buffaloes and they will stampede."

*****

The next morning, Mowgli took his animals to the river. Akela and Mowgli's wolf brother were waiting. "It's time, Mowgli. Shere Khan is looking for you near the river right now," said Akela.

"I'm ready. My buffaloes are in the river now. Let's begin the stampede," said Mowgli.

As Mowgli planned, the buffaloes saw the two big grey wolves and began to run. Shere Khan was busy looking for Mowgli and he didn't notice the stampede until it was too late. The old tiger tried to run, but he was not fast enough. The buffaloes crashed into him and the tiger disappeared under the water.

There was nothing left of the tiger except for his yellow tail!

Mowgli took the tail in his hands and said, "Shere Khan, our fight **is over**. You tried to take my life. Now, I'll take your tail."

Finally, Mowgli was safe from the evil tiger.

The old tiger tried to run, but he was not fast enough.

CHAPTER 12

The Hero's Return

A moment later, Buldeo, the hunter, appeared. "Boy, that tiger's tail is mine. Give it to me immediately. I'll give you two rupees for it," he said.

"Two rupees?" laughed Mowgli. "You'll give me two rupees for it, but you'll get 100 rupees from the British."

"That's not *your* tail. You didn't kill the tiger. Our buffaloes killed the tiger in the stampede, so the tail is *mine*!" shouted Buldeo and he **moved closer** to the boy. Then, he noticed the two big grey wolves and he was afraid.

Akela looked at the fat hunter. "Mowgli, what should we do? Is he dangerous?" he asked.

Mowgli laughed and said, "No, Akela, he's just a stupid man. Don't hurt him."

Buldeo saw Mowgli talking to the wolves and ran back to the village in a panic. Was the jungle boy possessed by a demon?

The wolves helped Mowgli find all the buffaloes. It took a long time and soon, it was time for Mowgli to return to the village.

The buffaloes were tired after the stampede. Mowgli walked back to the village with the wolves and the buffaloes. As he approached the village, he heard noises and saw lights. The boy thought to himself, "A celebration? Maybe it's for me. They want to thank me because I killed Shere Khan."

At the village, the people were waiting for Mowgli, but they didn't want to celebrate. "Wolf boy! Demon!" they shouted. "Go away!"

"We don't want you in our village!" somebody else shouted.

Buldeo shouted, "The boy is a demon. He walks with wolves and talks their language. He's also a **thief**. He stole my tiger's tail!"

Somebody threw a stone at Mowgli, and another person shot a gun. "What's this?" said Mowgli. "I killed the evil tiger. Why are you throwing stones at me?"

"Go away, wolf boy!" the priest shouted. "Return to the jungle!"

Mowgli was sad. He looked at the angry people and thought, "The wolves didn't want me because I'm a human, and the people don't want me because I'm a wolf. Where can I go?"

And then, Mowgli felt a soft **fur** nose touch his hand.

"These people are like our wolf pack," whispered Akela. "They're afraid of you because you're different. They don't want you here. Come, return with us to the jungle. You'll be safe now. Your enemy, Shere Khan, is dead."

Mowgli left the village and began to walk to the jungle. "Let's go, Akela," he said.

Suddenly, Mowgli heard a woman's voice. It was Messua.

"Nathos, Nathos! Wait!" she shouted. Messua ran towards Mowgli. "Oh, my son. My beautiful boy. They think you're a demon, but I don't believe them. I know you're good. Thank you for killing the evil tiger. Now, you must return to the jungle. You're not safe here."

"Goodbye, Messua," said Mowgli. "I'm returning to the jungle now. But I won't forget you. You were good to me."

"Look! Here's Shere Khan's tail," Mowgli said.

Mowgli and the two wolves walked all night and all day. It was evening when they arrived at the Council Rock. Then, Mowgli went to visit Mother Wolf.

"Mother, the humans don't want me in their village," he said. "But look! Here's Shere Khan's tail."

"Mowgli, I'm very impressed," said Mother Wolf. "I remember your first night in our cave. You looked like a little frog, but you were a brave, strong boy."

Suddenly, Mowgli heard a familiar voice. It was Bagheera!

"Good work, little brother," said Bagheera. "We **missed** you in the jungle. Come now, it's time to go to Council Rock."

Mowgli climbed up to the high rock and put the tiger's tail on the rock. Akela lay down next to the tail. All the other wolves came to Council Rock to see the tiger's tail. The wolves were weak and thin from eating bad food. Since the night of the fire, they didn't have a leader to teach them about the dangers of the jungle. Some wolves couldn't walk because of the thorns in their paws.

"We need a leader!" one wolf shouted. "Lead us, Mowgli! Lead us, Akela!"

"No!" said Bagheera. "It's too late. You wanted to kill Akela. You were ready to kill Mowgli. Now, you must learn to take care of yourselves."

Mowgli stood up and spoke, "You wolves sent me to the human village. Then, the humans sent me to the jungle. I'll hunt with Akela and my wolf brothers. Baloo and Bagheera will be my friends. I don't need you any more."

The next day, Mowgli left the pack with Baloo, Bagheera and his wolf brothers. It was time to start a new life.

It was time to start a new life.

CHAPTERS 11-12 ACTIVITIES

1 Find words in the puzzle to complete the sentences.

p	o	s	s	e	s	s	e	d
w	g	l	e	x	d	e	r	o
u	r	t	o	g	u	n	s	b
z	a	b	s	e	v	o	h	e
y	s	f	s	j	d	l	o	y
e	s	g	m	c	k	n	t	e
c	r	a	s	h	e	d	o	d

1. The driver lost control of the car and .... into a wall.
2. The hunter .... the tiger.
3. We sat on the .... , under a tree.
4. The animals .... the laws of the jungle.
5. The man killed his enemy with a ....
6. Evil spirits .... the boy.

Did you know?

The setting of *The Jungle Book* is the Pench Tiger Reserve in India. Many of the locations in the story are real places in the area, for example, the Wainganga River, Kanhiwara Village and the Seeonee Hills.

2 Look at the pictures. Then correct the sentences according to the story.

1. Mowgli takes the buffaloes up into the hills.
2. Akela and Buldeo frighten the buffaloes at the river.
3. Mowgli shows the tiger's tail to Buldeo.
4. The people in the village are happy to see Mowgli after he kills Shere Khan.

3 Answer the questions. Write the answers in your notebook.

1. On the first day of his job, how did Mowgli find out he was in danger?
2. Briefly describe Mowgli's plan to kill Shere Khan.
3. Who came to help the wolf brother with Mowgli's plan? Why?
4. Why did Buldeo run back to the village in a panic?
5. Why did Mowgli return to the jungle with Akela?
6. What did Mowgli decide to do at the end of the story?

GLOSSARY

English	Castellano	Català
alive	vivo	viu
anger	enfado	enuig
behave	comportarse	comportar-se
claws	garras	urpes, grapes
coals	brasas	brases
council	consejo	consell
deer	ciervo, venado	cérvol
didn't make sense	no tenían sentido	no tenien sentit
even	incluso	fins i tot
evil	malvado, perverso	malvat, pervers
fell asleep	se quedaron dormidos	van adormir-se
free	libres	lliures
from now on	de ahora en adelante	a partir d'ara, d'ara endavant
fur	peluda	peluda
gate	verja, puerta	reixat, porta
ground	suelo	terra
helpless	indefensas	indefenses
howled	aulló	va udolar
is over	ha terminado	ha acabat
laws	leyes	lleis
let's make a deal	hagamos un trato	fem un tracte
manners	modales	maneres, formes
missed	echamos de menos	vam trobar a faltar, vam enyorar
moved closer	se acercó	es va acostar
nodded his head	asintió con la cabeza	va assentir amb el cap
nuts	frutos secos	fruita seca
pack	manada	bandada

GLOSSARY

English	Euskara	Galego
alive	bizirik	vivo
anger	haserre	anoxo, enfado
behave	jokatzen	comportarse
claws	atzaparrak	poutas
coals	txingarrak, brasak	brasas
council	kontseilu	consello
deer	orein	cervo, veado
didn't make sense	ez zuten zentzurik	non tiñan sentido
even	ere	mesmo, incluso
evil	maltzur	malvado, perverso
fell asleep	lo hartu zuten	quedaron durmidos
free	askeak	libres
from now on	gaurtik aurrera	de agora en diante
fur	iletsu	peluda
gate	burdinesi	cancela, porta
ground	lur	chan
helpless	defentsarik gabeko	indefensas
howled	ulu egin zuen	ouveou, ouleou
is over	bukatu da	rematou
laws	legeak	leis
let's make a deal	egin dezagun tratua	fagamos un trato
manners	jokamoldeak	modais
missed	-en falta sumatu	facemos de menos
moved closer	hurbildu zen	achegouse
nodded his head	buruarekin baietsi zuen	asentiu coa cabeza
nuts	fruitu lehorrak	froitos secos
pack	talde	manda

GLOSSARY

English	Castellano	Català
path	camino	camí
paws	patas	potes
poisonous	venenosas	verinoses
pretended	fingían	fingien
proud	orgulloso	orgullós
pushed	metió; empujó	va ficar; va empènyer
raised	levantó	va aixecar, va alçar
roared	rugió	va rugir
roof	tejado	teulada
safe	a salvo; segura	fora de perill; segura
share	compartir	compartir
sharp	afilados	esmolades
shook his head	negó con la cabeza	va negar amb el cap
soft	suave	suau
stampede	huyen en desbandada	fugen a la desbandada
stay away	se alejara	s'allunyés
streams	arroyos	rierols
strength	fuerza	força
surrounded	rodearon a	van envoltar
take care of	cuidar de	tenir cura de
there was nothing left	no quedó nada	no hi va quedar res
thief	ladrón	lladre
thorns	espinas	espines
trust	fiar de, confiar en	refiar de, confiar en
turned	(se) volvió; giró; se dio la vuelta	(es) va girar, (es) va tombar

English	Euskara	Galego
path	bidexka	camiño
paws	erpeak	patas
poisonous	pozoitsuak	velenosas
pretended	plantak egiten zituzten	finxían
proud	harro	fachendoso, orgulloso
pushed	sartu zuen; bultzatu zituen	meteu; empurrou
raised	altxatu zuen	ergueu
roared	orro egin zuen	ruxiu
roof	teilatu	tellado
safe	arriskutik kanpo; seguru	san e salvo; segura
share	partekatzen, zatitzen	compartir, partillar
sharp	zorrotzak	afiados
shook his head	buruarekin ezetz esan zuen	negou coa cabeza
soft	leun	suave, mol
stampede	arrapaladan ihes egiten dute	foxen en desbandada
stay away	urrundu	afastase
streams	errekak	regueiros, arroios
strength	indar	forza
surrounded	inguratu zuten	rodearon a
take care of	zaintzen	coidar de, ter conta de
there was nothing left	ez zen ezer gelditu	non quedou nada
thief	lapur	ladrón
thorns	arantzak	espiñas
trust	-ekin fidatu	fiar de, confiar en
turned	jiratu zen; buelta eman zuen	volveu(se); xirou; deu(se) a volta

GLOSSARY

English	Castellano	Català
waste	perdáis; malgastaban	perdeu; malgastaven
whispered	susurraron	van xiuxiuejar
with pleasure	con mucho gusto	amb molt de gust
won't argue	no discutiré	no discutiré
worm	gusano	cuc

GLOSSARY

English	Euskara	Galego
waste	alferrik gal; xahutzen	perdades; desbaldían
whispered	xuxurlatu zuten	moumearon
with pleasure	gustu handiz	con moito gusto
won't argue	ez dut eztabaidatuko	non discutirei
worm	zizare	verme

SNAKE SCHOOL

If you visit a school of children from the Vadi tribe in the south of Gujarat, India, you'll notice the silence in the classrooms. The children are concentrating very hard. It isn't surprising, because in front of them is a lethal snake! These children are learning how to become **snake charmers**.

All Vadi children go to snake school from the age of two and spend ten years there. The boys learn to charm the snakes with a flute, and the girls learn to hold the snakes and **care for** them. The Vadi have got a lot of respect for their snakes. They never extract the snakes' **fangs**. They prefer to feed the cobras with a special herbal substance. This way, the snake's poison can't hurt anybody. After some time, the substance loses its effect. After seven months, the Vadi return the snakes to their natural habitat.

At the age of 12, the children are ready to follow in the ancient traditions of their tribe. These traditions started over 1,000 years ago with India's great Rajas (kings). In 1991, snake charming became illegal, but the Vadi tribe continues practising its traditions.

snake charmers	encantadores de serpientes	encantadors de serps	suge-sorgintzaileak	encantadores de serpes
care for	cuidar de	tenir cura de	zaindu	ter conta de
fangs	colmillos	ullals	letaginak	cairos, cabeiros

1 Use the words in the pot to complete the sentences.

1. The Vadi are a .... in India.
2. Today, snake charming is ....
3. The boys use a flute to .... the snakes.
4. The Vadi have got a lot of .... for their snakes.
5. Vadi children start snake school at the age of ....
6. The Vadi never keep a snake for more than .... months.

2 Complete the puzzle below.

Across ►

1. The … learn to care for the snakes.
4. In Vadi schools, there is … in the classrooms.
5. The Vadi treat their snakes with … .
6. At … , Vadi children learn how to be snake charmers.

Down ▼

2. Another word for India's great kings.
3. They use a special … substance against the snake's poison.

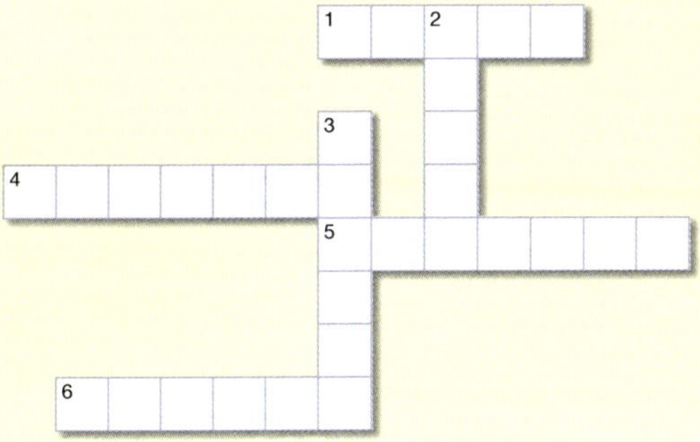

A SNAKE LEGEND

More than 270 species of snakes inhabit India. But in some countries, like Ireland, you can only find them at the zoo! According to legend, in the 5th century, St Patrick stood on a hill and used a stick to send all the snakes into the sea.

But the absence of native snakes in Ireland isn't because of St Patrick. There's a scientific explanation for this phenomenon. Millions of years ago, the world consisted of super-continents before the land broke up into separate countries. According to scientists, snakes **evolved** on one of these super-continents about 100 million years ago. Later, the continent broke up and the creatures made their way by land to other countries, including England and Scotland. But they couldn't get to Ireland, because at that time it was under the sea.

Today, you can find snakes in deserts, forests, mountains and seas in most areas of the world except for Ireland, New Zealand, Iceland, Greenland and Antarctica. All these places are surrounded by water. So, it seems that snakes don't change their habitat if they must cross the sea to do so.

evolved evolucionaron van evolucionar eboluzionatu zuten evolucionaron

3 Match the questions and answers. Look at the numbers and letters. Then colour the correct section in the puzzle in green to find the Irish national emblem.

1. Where are Ireland's only snakes?
2. What's the Irish legend about snakes?
3. Where did snakes evolve?
4. What happened to Ireland millions of years ago?
5. Which other areas don't have snakes?
6. Why aren't there any native snakes in Ireland?

.... a. On one of the super-continents.

.... b. New Zealand, Iceland, Greenland and Antarctica.

.... c. Because they don't cross the sea to change their habitat.

.... d. St Patrick sent all the snakes into the sea.

.... e. The country was under the sea.

.... f. At the zoo.

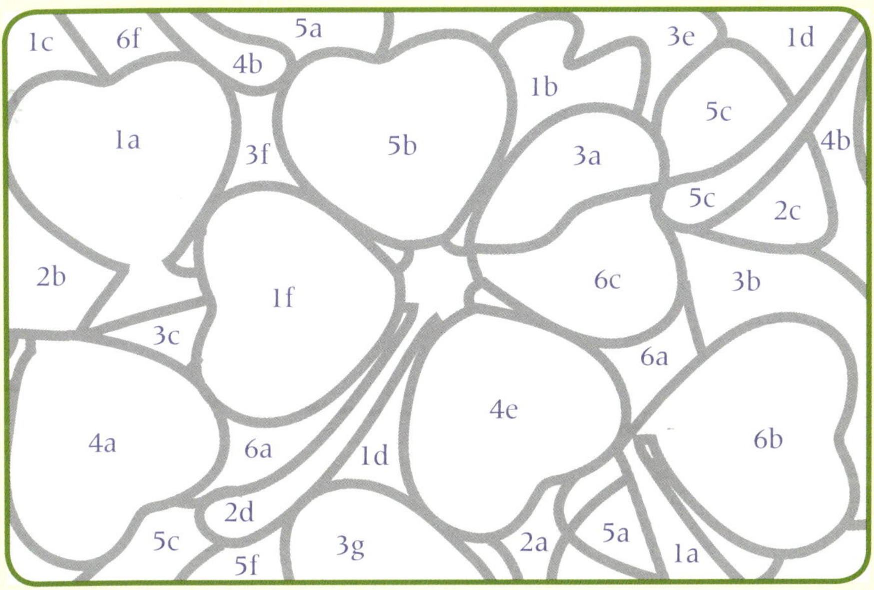

MINI TASK

Most people are afraid of snakes, but snakes are useful creatures. Use the Internet to find information about how snakes help the environment. Use the information you find to make a poster.